D1516563

the little guide to

light-filled mornings

THIRTY DAYS TO GREATER JOY & PURPOSE

custom illustrations: emmaline fleener

ISBN: 9781658042178
library of congress control number: 2020902156

the little guide to
light-filled mornings

THIRTY DAYS TO GREATER JOY & PURPOSE

CAITLIN SHEA MCCOY

To Sam & Sadie:
May you always know mornings and days that are true to you and your sense of wonder.

INTRODUCTION

Hello, morning.
Nice to see you.
It's glorious to be here.

These are the things I say many mornings, when I wake up and the world seems bright of its own accord.

Hello, morning.
Everything feels wrong.
Please show me how to know it's ok.

These are the things I say some mornings, when I wake up and the world seems to have lost its luster (and it usually feels like my fault).

After years of feeling like everything was up to chance and like I had no control over my life—or worse, I did but shouldn't be trusted with it—I did what any girl would do: I panicked.

It's a portion of my life I'd like to gloss over, but like most things in life, the only way was through.

There were days when I didn't know how I would stand to live another, even though I always smiled back at the person at the grocery store, even though I became accustomed to pretending to be all right. And when I could no longer pretend, again, I did what any girl would do: I surrendered to it.

And in doing so, I allowed myself to hope: that maybe, just maybe, there was a way out of the fears that had come to crowd in my daily life. And of course, there was.

And the way out started very, very early each morning—before anyone else was awake.

This is your little guide to light-filled mornings.

I trust that you'll use it well—dog-earing pages here and there, jotting down ideas in the margins... fully using it up, each day, because that's what it's here for.

That being said, I have a confession to make: As well-intentioned as I am for creating a set of morning routines that will set you up for a life beyond your wildest hopes and dreams, I can't tell you what's right for you. I couldn't possibly know exactly what will make your heart sing. Oh, I can take plenty of great guesses. I can tell you what's worked for me. I can tell you stories of what's worked for other people. The good news here is that only you know what's best for you. Read that again: you know what's best for you.

And because you are you, and are there everywhere you go, you hold each and every key and resource you'd ever need to find your way on this journey—this journey to greater self-awareness and joy that comes from finding time to align for your day before you set foot out of your home.

The idea of alignment is really quite simple: there's you, consciously reading each word on the page. And then there's You, the real, true, deeper part of you, under any layers of identity you've taken on through the years.

There's a Caitlin who is the author of this book, who was really afraid for a long time that she'd never write a book or even get her journalism degree, but did, and who really loves coffee, maybe a little too much, and highlights her hair blonde because she can't bear to be without the identity of a blonde even though it's rather brown now, as the years have gone on, and loves chihuahuas and period pieces and musicals and tattoos and also candles and lists of things.

There's also a Caitlin who is at peace with who she truly is, at all times, in everything, with a deep and true knowing that all is well, all the time. And there's a You like that as well.

Now, when you're in alignment, those two you's are one. You can love your coffee and identities and all the things and know, truly, that all is well, all the time, in the here and now. You and you are in sync. And you know because you feel wonderful.

The process of experiencing light-filled mornings is not another task to add to your already-full to-do list. It's about finding the things to do that inspire the way to be fully aligned—where you meet You. And that is a beautiful thing.

In the course of my travels through life with light-filled mornings, I've discovered that the ideal aligning morning typically has an element that is cozy, movement-oriented, or feels inspired. I love to have elements of all three within my morning.

I encourage you to take this one day at a time—indeed, one moment at a time is all we ever have—and let yourself savor this book in that way. The first three parts of the book have been set up to read over the course of 30 days, which is a glorious amount of time to set aside to show yourself how very capable you are of taking time for yourself, just because it feels good to do so. And life is a lot better when you feel good. For you, and everyone else. *Here's to a beautiful journey, dear friend.*

*"There's nothing as cozy as a piece of candy
and a book."*
– BETTY MACDONALD

PART I
c o z y

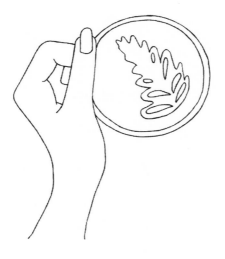

The cornerstone of any transformation is safety.
It sounds counter-intuitive; isn't transformation in your day, your life, about risk? Feeling the fear and doing it anyway?

On some level, yes. But we have to feel safe—on a fundamental level—in order to see that we can take the risk, do the thing, make the time, take the leap.

To feel cozy in your space, in your home, in your little corner of the world, is the first step.

Day One.
Good morning.
You're here.
Hello.

There is something so freeing in solitude. Awake before everyone else, or even just in your own corner of a room—in your own world you've made space for.

It's when we've made the breathing room to be alone that we can most easily see that we're all connected.

And so this morning, let's start with a breath of connection; today, connection to yourself.

Take a deep breath in and hold for five counts. Let that deep breath all the way out.
Let's go again.
In for five... out for five.

And now: take out a trusted journal, scribble on this page, type out on your computer or phone, or just quietly think to yourself.

When was the last time I felt safe to feel pure, unbridled joy?

When was the last time I felt completely free?

Let those questions sit with you. And then, see what you can bring into this morning—yes, right now—that feels like that.

cozy means—

A quiet mug of steaming hot coffee, the steam rising off the hot liquid in early morning golden light

A favorite plush robe (in your favorite color)

Ridiculously thick socks in the winter

Anything that can sink or squash when you sit on it

Day Two.

If waking up a little earlier is still new, you're likely tired today. When you're still in the fog of waking up, and perhaps the light isn't even over the horizon yet, what better time to sink into coziness?

Do you have a mug of your favorite hot (or cool) drink? If not, go get one. This is your time to be cozy and there is no rush.

Even if this morning hasn't gone as planned thus far, you are making time, however much there is, and there is always the opportunity for it to feel cushy and luxurious.

Take your five deep breaths in. Let those five deep breaths out.
Let's go again. Five in, five out.

What did you do with your morning time yesterday? If it felt deliciously cozy and delightful, have a go at it again.

In addition, today, read something other than this book.

If your feelings of joy and freedom yesterday were in reading a book, great! Go grab it.

If not, make time this morning to read: the bestseller on your nightstand you're loving, the email newsletter you have been saving in your inbox but haven't gotten a chance to read yet, the newest issue of the magazine you love that came in the mail, a catalog of beautiful things, some exquisite coffee packaging with clever marketing copy on the back.

Just read something you think will make you feel joy, hope, freedom. Today, you are under no moral obligation to read the news or things you think you "should" like or "should" be reading, for whatever reason. *This is your cozy, light-filled morning. Fill it with the light inside.*

cozy means—

A hardback book with the really nice, matte book jacket

Inhaling your coffee beans really deeply, in a way that would make others stare if they were around

A fuzzy pet curled up in your lap, with no care in the world because you are there

Remembering the delightful thing your friend said so well the other day and relishing in the hilarity of it

Day Three.
Good morning.

The lovely thing about making time each morning to do something that you love (or are curious enough to see if you love it) is that each day builds upon another.

If you've invested in reading a book and have made time each day to read it and are enjoying it, that's fantastic.

If you've invested in cozying up with a wool blanket, regardless of weather, with a mug of coffee, and just staring out the window—also fantastic.

It's your third day of making your time a priority; what can you feel building? If you feel hope and ease building, relish in that feeling. Really soak it up. Like a bubble bath of good-feeling, lightheartedness, that you can feel bubbling to the surface of your being.

If you feel sleep deprivation and time anxiety building, let's feel it—and see what good things these feelings are trying to bring you instead.

It's incredible how much to-do lists bring a feeling of rushed panic... even in the control of them. We feel we're being productive; when in fact, we're often so wrapped up in the thinking-of-doing-the-things rather than doing-the-things that we're just robbing our joy of this moment, here, now.

The universe isn't in a rush; you are. What will unfold will unfold, in its time. You're on a grand, highly personal experiment of mornings right now. Consciously allow yourself to make more room in your awareness and your world for this cozy time you've gifted yourself.

Breaths in, breaths out. You're doing so well.

cozy means—

A really delightful quote that makes you feel like the author "gets" you on another level

Watching squirrels play outside your window, making time to notice their swishy tails

A chill playlist that feels like a hug and headphones that block all other noise

Grocery store flowers on your kitchen table that have amazing texture and fluffiness to the bouquet, all for less than $10

Day Four.
This morning, let it be.

Just spend a few minutes, letting it just be.

Whatever "it" is.

Listen to whatever noises are around you; the wind, the birds chirping, the dryer going, the air conditioner, the heating vent.

Not reacting; not judging; just being.

You are loved.
You are held.
You are supported.

The songbird outside is singing for you.

And all you have to do this morning is be.

cozy means—

Curled up lying in bed with clean, fresh sheets and your favorite blanket pulled up to your head with just your nose peeking out

Deep breaths, calming mind and body

Wearing your favorite sweater

Seeing your loved ones' faces in photos around your home

Day Five.

This morning, get cozy with smells.

All of our senses crave to be held, loved, and supported, and comforted in some way.

The sense of smell can be wonderfully comforting. Think of smells that make you feel cozy. Cinnamon? Fresh laundry? If you have an essential oils diffuser, get it running for your cozy morning.

If you'd like to light a candle, do so.

Orange rinds and cardamom in hot water on the stove can be equally effective.

How have smells impacted you this morning?

Where could you see them boosting your day in surprising ways?

cozy means—

The smell of sweet spices encircling your space

The feel of flower petals

Reversible sequins and the feelings they bring

Very hot water—baths, hot tubs, dish water that turns into a pleasant experience

Day Six.
Let's acknowledge you woke up feeling good this morning.

You're going to keep building on that—to stay in that soft, cozy, snuggly place. Grab the nearest blanket or throw and wrap it around yourself.

Close your eyes, take a nice, deep breath, and say to yourself:
"I'm proud I'm letting myself feel good."

"I'm going to take this good feeling with me through my day."

Doesn't it feel good to feel good?

cozy means—

A large pot of oatmeal on the stove

Wool tassels on favorite throw blankets and pillows

Being surrounded by low, warm lighting

The feeling of a rough-fabric-but-still-favorite quilt

Day Seven.
You've been spending dedicated time to being cozy for an entire week now.

Feel free to revel in rest this morning.

You could go back to bed, if you'd like.

You could watch a favorite show on TV under a blanket.

What feels like the most restful, cozy thing you could do today? The first thing that pops into your head—do it. Don't second guess. You know best.

cozy means—

Sketching paper and colored pencils to doodle

Yarn and knitting needles for a new handmade project

A large dark chocolate candy bar—bonus points if there are flecks of fruit inside

The feel of getting "your table" at your favorite coffeeshop

Day Eight.

You've practiced being cozy solo—which is the foundation for having a lovely day that feels like a hug "out" in the world.

If it feels fun to you, today is a great day to pull another in.

Invite a friend out to your favorite coffeeshop on the fly; or go visit one and see if you make a new friend, even if it's just with the barista. Especially if it's with the barista.

Creating cozy moments in your own home and safe space are so important. Building on that to take the cozy, good-feeling being out with you in places you frequent is the next step.

Because truly, you can cultivate a cozy light-filled morning anywhere, once you're practiced.

Today's affirmation: *I bring cozy with me wherever I go.*

Bring this with you through the day.

cozy means—

Avocado toast complete with a fried egg atop and just the right pinch of salt and pepper

Slowing down your morning to appreciate life

Warm and calming colors—on clothing, blankets, walls

Saying hello to the morning sun

Day Nine.
Cozy can be creative.

Reveling in the coziness of your morning is the perfect jumping-off point for creativity to flow.

If you have an adult (or goodness, even a children's, if you can get away with it) coloring book, get it out with some colored pencils.

Or just get a piece of printer paper out and go to town with a pencil, just scribbling and doodling wherever your hand wants to take it.

If you're a sewer or a crafter, get some projects out now.

Wherever your natural creativity wants to take you, let it flow there now.

cozy means—

Becoming your own best friend, offering yourself encouragement and care

Cuddling with any person or creature you love to cuddle with

Being surrounded by your favorite souvenirs from travels

The smell of a freshly-sharpened No. 2 pencil

Day Ten.
Decide that nothing is more important than starting your day off feeling cozy—like you've been hugged from within and you're safe and comforted to find the fun of life.

Try a cozy affirmation today to ground yourself in safe, calm comfort.

Take a deep breath. Let it out.

Let's do it again. Take a deep breath. Let it out.

Three time's the charm: take a deep breath. Let it all the way out.

Say to yourself:
"I am safe. I am at peace. I am cozy."

"Wherever I go, whatever I do, whoever I'm with. I am safe. I am at peace. I am cozy."

Repeat to yourself, slowly, more and more surely, 10 times. It's day 10 of this journey, after all.

And when you're ready to do whatever it is that you do next—whether it's brushing your teeth, getting your favorite outfit out of the closet, or getting in the car for your commute—bring that cozy with you.

You are safe. You are at peace. You are cozy.
Wherever you go, whatever you do, and whoever you're with today—you can bring that cozy with you.

cozy means—

Textures, many of them, layered one upon another

Nature brought indoors, like house plants or even found acorns

A chess board, checkers, or a deck of cards for quiet fun

The sound of light rain against window panes and feeling safe and dry inside

A Little Cozy Story

I've interviewed a lot of women on how their cozy mornings look; and the beautiful thing is that none of them look exactly the same. And why would they? This whole life thing; it's a personal journey.

Here's Autumn's cozy story:

"I wake up with kids in my bed," Autumn laughs. Autumn homeschools her children and wakes up when they do, generally. "Most of our day is following their lead, and their interests... it's very open, flowy, and easy," she says. "So while we have a rhythm, there's nothing rigid, and no set schedule, which helps me keep less stressed... if I have no schedule, we can't be late."

In the mornings, she and the children will make breakfast—"usually smoothies or oatmeal and always coffee for me"—and have time for reading to start the day slowly.

"I'll often get my journal out while they have time with their books," Autumn says. Then they all wash up. "They brush their hair and teeth, wash their face, I'll do my morning beauty routine... and then if it's nice out, we'll go outside for a while and take lots of deep breaths out there and play. We go with the flow as long as it's fun. I've had to train myself to be easygoing... I have my moments, of course, but if I'm stressed, I always apologize. It's important to teach them that even if we lose our temper, we can be sorry, admit we make mistakes, and that's ok."

"Mornings are when I set my intentions for the day; my attitude for the day, the headspace I want to be in, it's the perfect time to take whatever time I need to meditate, move my body... literally whatever it is that I need. I used to be go-go-go with the kids, but when I take this time, I am so much better being able to communicate and be present with them... mornings and bedtimes are the grounding experiences. We base a lot of our homeschooling on the Waldorf method, which says a child's day begins with bedtime... how you put them to bed impacts their day when they wake up. So as much as we have a rhythm to our mornings, we also have a rhythm at bedtime—with stories, being tucked in, kisses and hugs, and time together. It's so important to take those moments."

"All that is important is this one moment in movement. Make the moment important, vital, and worth living. Do not let it slip away unnoticed and unused."

- MARTHA GRAHAM

PART II
movement

Small children are always standing on their toes.
Up and down, up and down, toe-walking, hopping, bouncing—in line for the grocery checkout as much as the moment they wake up, sleepy-eyed and wild-haired. Living a life in which movement is a natural course enlivens every moment of your day.

Day Eleven.
We're shaking things up this morning, quite literally.

Movement in the morning can be so pivotal to the quality of your day—even if you don't necessarily feel like taking a jog outdoors or doing anything intensive.

That's where questioning what movement feels best to you will come in handy.

Ask yourself: ***when was the last time moving felt really good?***

Was it a challenging, sweat-inducing cardio workout you streamed?

Was it ballet class as a child?

Was it a group class, spent getting to know active community members?

Spend some time reflecting; and then do as much of that thing as you can this morning.

Even if it's some light stretches while booking a fitness class for later—or just light stretches.

Just get it flowing.

movement means—

Going up and down on the balls of your feet

Pyramid stretch in between work calls

Walking across the room for more coffee

A run through the park on a sunny day

Day Twelve.
Movement isn't difficult. Did you know that?

So often, we make it difficult. We think of movement in terms of reps and gym time and cardio and rules.

But there are no rules.

Movement is natural... it's so natural, it's as natural to breathe. When we're present in our bodies, grounded to the earth, life becomes a dance.

Today, think about how incredibly easy movement could be if you felt connected to the very ground you move on.

Take a seat, if you haven't already, and take a nice, deep, letting-go breath and picture how very connected you are to the earth. Your feet are on the floor, I'd imagine, and not the prickly grass.

In a moment, I'd like you to close your eyes and envision the most perfect earthen floor you could ever envision.

Maybe it's soft, bright green grass. Maybe it's a bed of flowers that won't crumple when you step on them. Maybe it's sand, from a beach. Whatever it is, imagine that, right now. Really feel how it would feel to have your feet sitting within that earthen floor.

Now, give yourself permission to connect to that perfect earthen floor all day long—because it's there to support you, movement by movement. Anytime throughout the day that you start to feel brain fog, disconnected, sore from a workout, or are simply aware of a disconnect, just take a deep breath and reconnect to that perfect earthen floor.

movement means—

Yoga class with your best friend

Yoga class with a brand-new friend you met at yoga class

Dancing to your favorite movie soundtrack

Skipping with a small child across the street, hand in hand

Day Thirteen.
Are you doing movement you love? Are you connected to your perfect earthen floor? Fantastic.

Look at you, 13 days in and doing so very well! I'm seriously proud of you for showing up for yourself in this way and you have full permission to be proud of yourself, too.

Today, think of how movement is really taking you from now to now. And now. And now. Each moment, everything around is in a flurry of movement—our bodies, our thoughts, each and every atom in each and every piece of furniture, each strike on a keyboard key.

As Einstein showed, energy is mass, and mass is energy—moving, vibrating energy is all around us and a part of us, always.

Movement is inherent in all we do, experience, and touch. And so you may choose to do a special workout today, or go for a walk, or just have a little skip on your step when you go from your car into the store.

It's all just taking you from now to now—and it's there for you to enjoy.

movement means—

Elliptical machine time while watching your favorite show

Hula-hooping on the lawn

Throwing a kettle ball back and forth, feet against a friend's

Dribbling a soccer ball across an open field

Day Fourteen.
Are you having fun yet? Today's movement is super special.

Are you ready?

If you have a yoga mat, go grab it and roll it out. If not, get comfy in a special spot on the floor in whatever position is most comfortable for you.

Take a nice, deep, letting-go breath, and bring your arms overhead, and then down. Do this again. One more time. Ahhh. Doesn't that feel nice? Now, imagine that all your presence is inside your body.

You're not thinking of what you'll do when this is over (and if you are, you're politely telling that thought to wait its turn).

Really envision your own powerful presence right behind the center of your head, right behind your eyes. Call it all in.

Feel how very movement-oriented you are, even when sitting, lying, or standing, in stillness.

And now, take a nice, deep, letting-go breath, and bring your arms overhead, and then down.
Do this again.
One more time.

And that's it!

Enjoy your day, movement to movement, moment to moment.

movement means—

Jogging alongside your furry best friend

Dancing to musical soundtracks with headphones on, complete with jumps and twirls

Biking through a cluster of trees, leaves falling slowly around you

Pilates on your yoga mat, in the center of the living room floor

Day Fifteen.
We live in a day and age where it's possible to stream any workout we could imagine in our living room, which is a beautiful thing.

If it's raining outside, you can still do your favorite Pilates routine on your very own carpet.

However, sometimes it can be really fun to get outside.

Ask yourself: ***when was the last time I truly enjoyed being outside?***

When was the last time I truly enjoyed moving outside?

Was it a walk, a hike, or yoga in the park? Something else entirely?

Whether it's today or later this week, make a promise to yourself to get outside and move in whatever way sounds the most fun to you. Not like the most endurance-testing thing or the most convenient thing—unless those things sound fun.

Whatever comes to you and you feel most enthusiastic about, write down here or on a page in your journal. Now it's time to promise yourself you'll allow the time for it. I'm so excited for you!

movement means—

Squats while your morning smoothie blends

Surfing of a morning in the ocean

Surfing of a morning on your couch with kids or pets to laugh with you

Handstands with feet against the wall

Day Sixteen.
Have you noticed our emotions move as well as our physical bodies? It's a fun time, being a human.

It can take an incredible amount of energy to move an emotion, intentionally.

I'd like for you, this morning, to feel into whatever you're authentically feeling, right now, in this moment. And really let yourself feel that.

And if it's buoyantly happy and joyful, at peace, or anything that makes you feel wonderful, fantastic. Keep that going.

And if it's not something that makes you feel wonderful, it's a good time to get curious.

Ask yourself: *why is this here? What is it trying to show me?*

Let that emotion know you see it and you're thankful for its messages. Our emotions are always trying to guide us back to alignment.

And you can, slowly, gently, but surely, move emotions that don't feel so good to emotions that do. Sometimes a walk is all it takes. Sometimes it's just telling that emotion that you saw it and it's safe to move.

Know that you are safe to move today—your body, and your emotions.

Take a deep breath and greet your day.

movement means—

Break dancing in the street, waiting for the subway, waiting for the microwave to ding

That stretch you do back and forth when you've been sitting at your laptop too long

Moving books from the shelf to the table to read

Vacuuming with flair

Day Seventeen.
Dance. Party.

This morning is dance party day.

In the words of ABBA, "you are the dancing queen, young and sweet, only seventeen"... days into your light-filled mornings journey.

And while I don't believe you truly need to earn a dance party (it seems like a very obvious gift inherent to being human), you have definitely earned a morning dance party. If children or significant others will be awakened by loud, audible music, please wear headphones.

If there's no one around to wake up or they want to partake, too, put on the ultimate feel-good song, whatever that is for you.

And now, dance, for the length of the song, the album, the playlist—whatever it is that lights you up and you've made time for.

Doesn't it feel good?

movement means—

Karaoke with all the hand motions and hip shakes

Brushing your teeth while also bopping around

Having the time of your life, from now to now

Being alive

Day Eighteen.

A lot of movement centers around moving forward.

For example, we'll pedal our bikes forward... we'll do crunches, sitting up, knowing we're moving forward towards a goal of more core strength... walking TO a location, rather than FROM a location.

Today I'd like you to really process what it means to be moving forward—always to your highest good.

This is your morning, and your day, and your life. And you can't go back. Only forward.

And that, in itself, is a very good thing.

movement means—

Reliving marching band days, moving your fingers to the B flat scale even without your instrument in hand

Watering house plants while also pointing your toes

Moving forward, in every thought and action you take

Skiing down a mountainside on vacation

Day Nineteen.

Resistance is a big thing when it comes to toning our muscles. We use resistance bands in Pilates to get a little extra stretch; a little extra pull.

We push away from the floor to complete a push up. Resistance is an essential part of movement; but how much better is it to realize that instead of merely resisting what comes our way, we can also begin reaching to the things that we want?

When you use hand weights in a workout, think more about how you can reach those arms instead of resisting the weight coming back in to be felt in the muscles.

When you think of moving forward and what movement and this journey means to you, think of where you can stop resisting and start reaching.

movement means—

Walking towards a higher calling in life

Scrolling through Pinterest with vigor and enthusiasm

Knee jumps that make you remember your core strength

Starring in the movie of your life, making each frame full of the movements that feel good

Day Twenty.
Today, just move. In whatever way feels best.

It could be a gentle stretch; it could be part of a workout program; it could be a brief walk or ride, even.

Just make the move.

In whatever way feels best.

Give yourself the space to know what that is.

And just do it. For you.

movement means—

Cannon ball in the pool

Canoeing on the lake, sun glittering down on the water

That brief moment between the jump and landing

Anything that makes your soul feel like it's on fire, in the best way

A Little Movement Story

Movement, as we've seen, can be defined in so many ways. While I've interviewed a lot of women who make space for movement in their mornings, one story that stood out to share was that of Aishwarya's—a poet who demonstrates very well the movement of time, space, and word.

Here's Aishwarya's movement story:

"I have this friend who is a sticker poet, and they gave me a bunch of their stickers to just have for myself, but I put them in the neighborhood I live in," Aishwarya says. "My neighborhood is super isolated, so I thought, I am just going to put a bunch of stickers up and brighten the neighborhood's day. "

"By mid-afternoon, if I feel myself getting sleepy, I think, you know what, I'm going to go take a walk. I go put out stickers... and now I love going for walks, and with the hills in Seattle, I don't have to go on an actual hike to get my cardio in! Just a 15 minute walk, and I'm done for the day," she laughs.

"I still do yoga, but walking for 15 minutes there and back, putting up stickers... most people won't see it, but someone will, and maybe it will make them happy. Maybe it won't. But you have to try. That's the only thing."

"There are only two ways to live your life. One is as though nothing is a miracle. The other is as though everything is a miracle."

– ALBERT EINSTEIN

PART III
inspired

What is a miracle in your life?
Could it be as simple as the way you choose to look at things? Without upliftment, life becomes drudgery—and while an occasional drudge is part of life, the best promise life holds is that a miracle is around each corner. To feel inspired in your life is a fundamental guiding light in having a life that inspires.

Day Twenty-one.
The first step to inspiration is really awareness.

Truly, we can't be aware of inspiration until we're aware, generally—of ourselves, of how we feel, of what it means to feel open or closed-off.

Over the past 20 days, you've probably been very aware of things you hadn't been for quite some time, if not ever. Even very small things have suddenly become that much more noticeable.

Becoming self-aware—of the thoughts that we think, the actions that we take, the beliefs that we hold, and the world that only we live in—that's the basis for today.

Write, either on this page or in your journal (or even a sticky note or random napkin!), answers to the following prompts:

When was the last time I felt truly inspired?

How do I know?

In what ways can I become truly inspired today?

Make space for the answers to come. Take all the time that you need. Some of the answers may trickle in, in deeper meaning and significance, throughout the day. That's a true hallmark of inspiration: it builds.

inspired means—

Feeling as though anything is possible

Social media captions that resonate

The exact book you were looking for at exactly the right moment

Serendipity

Day Twenty-two.

How do we know if an idea is inspired?

It's a word we use quite frequently; but do we know what it means to us?

"That painting is truly inspired!"

"Oh, thanks, I was inspired by those flowers... and Monet... and my favorite little dog."

What does it all mean?

The dictionary defines inspired as "aroused, animated, or imbued with the spirit to do something, by or as if by, a supernatural or divine influence."

A secondary definition says, "inhaled, inspired air."

Both definitions very accurately describe the hand of inspiration within my own life—but I want you to define it for yourself.

Today, vow to be inspired by inspiration itself.

Write in a trusty journal or on this page, your own definition.

To me, inspired is:

inspired means—

Bursting at the seams with an idea that's ready to pop

Taking a rest from doing for others and doing any hobby for yourself

Working with your hands to give to others

Lighting a candle and watching the flame come to life

Day Twenty-three.

Inspiration may be found anywhere: at the grocery store, on the back of a soda can, in a specific shade of yellow, in a really, really good novel, or even in a friend's latest story.

In the morning, though, it's a good idea to try **receiving** inspiration rather than going out to discover it.

In doing so, we're no longer on a quest to try and find something; we're just here, being ourselves, in alignment, and we're ready whenever inspiration is.

Inspiration can be quiet. It often whispers rather than shouts.

Sometimes it's accompanied by a ringing of the ears, and necessitates waiting a moment to see—is that really the voice of inspiration? Very often, it is.

This morning, I want you to be very cozy. I hope you've moved a little, even if it was to go from your bed to this spot, now, to gain inspiration.

And now—spend as long as you can, just sitting quietly.

Take a deep, letting-go breath, and let inspiration know that you're here. If you have a question for your own source of inspiration, go ahead and ask. And then wait, not rushing, not forcing, not anxiously anticipating—just wait.

And be sure to write down—here or in your journal or Notes app—whatever comes to you.

inspired means—

Journaling page after page, letting it flow

Coloring books that take hours to fill in the details but feel like it's just minutes

A feeling of "yes"

Surprise, with a deep knowing that it's a good surprise

Day Twenty-four.
To be inspired consistently, we really have to loosen up a little and let go of our fears.

Fear is much like an angry, impatient toddler that would very much like to get his or her way. This toddler is truly trying to do what's best for you—but how can they know what's best for you?

They're trying to rule with the insight of a toddler. Everything is big and scary and too itchy or the wrong color.

This morning, take a nice, deep, letting-go breath, and get real about your fears. Question them. Look them right in the face. They're not actually scary at all. They're just trying to protect you.

Write down, here or on paper, what it is that fear is trying to tell you.

Now question that. ***Is this valid for me?***

Very likely it's not. And if it is, I encourage you to go deeper.

Because you can trust in yourself. And this life. And this morning.

Your mantra, if it resonates, to take with you throughout the day: ***I trust in this moment. I release my fears.***

You're all set for a beautiful day.

inspired means—

Permission to be the true you, always, always

Good news delivered in a great way

Truth, peace, love and the feelings they bring

Brush strokes on a canvas

Day Twenty-five.
With inspiration, choosing from this now moment is all that really matters.

We may have been inspired several years ago by something, but it warrants checking in on from time to time.

And from that choice, let's open the playing field.

What if you just knew that anything was possible?

What do you feel inspired to do, in this now moment?

Just ask. The answers are there.

It just takes some practice, listening and following.

inspired means—

Your friends' artwork

Being the new person at the new book club and feeling at home

Birthday wishes, resolutions anytime of the year, intentions that make you smile

Continually surpassing what you previously thought possible

Day Twenty-six.
You are on this earth for a reason. Did you know?

Everyone's reason and purpose looks different to them; I personally feel that reason is to experience life, in joy.

It's easy for purpose to fuel inspiration; it's also quite easy for your sense of purpose to stamp out your sense of wonder.

Today, I invite you to begin to spend more time on that very special sense of wonder. You see, wonder is taking a thing you've seen a million times and saying, "Oh. I never noticed that." Wonder is saying, "what if... " Wonder is realizing that there is a second side, an opportunity for a closer look, and possibly something in our peripheral vision that's just gone unseen.

This morning, sitting in the exact place you are right now, write down, on this page or another paper, 26 things that you notice.

And then, really, truly take a closer look.

What do you appreciate about these elements?

Carry this sense of wonder throughout your day.

inspired means—

Violins playing in the next room, in real time or recorded

Revolutions of love and of heart

Revolutions of the sun and the earth

Making lists and feeling surprised by the amount of things to be grateful for on them

Day Twenty-seven.
The environments we're in, and how we see them, are often a reflection of just how inspired we feel on a day to day basis.

Today, I'd like you to look around in your morning environment:

What inspires you about this space?

What could make room for even more inspiration to flow in this space?

Write down the answers that come to you; either here or in a journal or other paper.

inspired means—

Names that just come to you: of businesses, pets, plants, anything

Multifaceted interests... and the passion to pursue them

Adventures full of excitement and twists and turns

Normal days you realize are suddenly full of excitement and twists and turns

Day Twenty-eight.
What if nothing went according to plan—and yet, everything fell into place?

When we open ourselves up to inspiration and follow its call, we're often venturing into what feels like the wild unknowns of life.

Inspiration can ask us to do many interesting things that may not make sense to our conscious mind. Sometimes, I turn left instead of right, even though it's the longer way around.

I once found a job I didn't know I wanted because I had a vivid dream that my local college was the answer to all of my problems.

I then quit that same job because I'd seen a certain number of snakes. (And had a higher-paying, better situation within four days.)

I started Light-filled Mornings because I heard the phrase in my mind and just knew.

We can plan all day long; and yet, the call of inspiration offers us so much more than we could ever conceive of. And when you're cozy, and you've moved, and you've opened yourself up to inspiration's song—things get interesting.

So if you're feeling twisted and turned, just know: it's a fun ride. You just have to let it be.

inspired means—

Asking for signs and seeing them in multitudes

Personalized keychains with your name spelled the right way at the gas station for the first time

Being silly, because silliness is just as important as seriousness sometimes

Feeling good just for the sake of feeling good

Day Twenty-nine.

You've made it so far on this journey; and I hope you are seeing, this very moment, this very morning, how very important it is to commit to yourself.

You're truly your longest-standing commitment; and so why shouldn't you be a priority? (Hint: you totally should.)

And beyond being committed, I know you see how much courage it takes to take the time for yourself each morning.

To say no to perceived obligations. To paint, sketch, journal, walk, snuggle in a blanket, or even just sit in stillness when there seems to be a lack of time running rampant in society.

Today, I know you can see your own courage. How you've taken each step, willingly, for yourself. Opened daily to inspiration and the unknown—and maybe even revisited the known that's been away for a while.

Bask in your courage this morning.
And take it out in your inspired day.

inspired means—

Documentaries that give you goosebumps, in a good way

Meeting the right person at the right time for the right reasons

Splashing in puddles and seeing your reflection

A tune you can't get out of your head

Day Thirty.

Did you know that the light within you shines through you?

You were born that way. Just like the morning sun comes up, no thought of blinders or dimming, so you shine from within, when you let yourself.

Light-filled mornings are about letting yourself shine. There is no forcing, no projection, because when there's nothing dampening that light, it simply is, as the sun within. It's not something to do, it's allowing to be; but sometimes the doing reminds the being.

And so, remember that this adventure won't ever truly be complete, and that in itself is a very good thing—because your light won't ever go out.

In these past thirty days, you've set the foundation, the early morning hour, of the days that make your life. And I know that looking around you, there are beautiful things to notice.

And one of those things to notice is how you are truly inspired, from within.

Today, let yourself shine.
Give yourself permission to do so all day long.
You're living light-filled mornings.

inspired means—

Saying "come to me," and letting the ideas flow

Loosening up and letting it be light

Making the phone call the instant you think to do it

Remembering movies you watched as a child and how limitless they made you feel

A Little Inspired Story

Inspiration likes to talk to us, to find us, in many different ways. It can be found in a song on the radio, a book that gives you goosebumps, and perhaps most often, in just being. Simply being. That gives it the space to find you. I love how everyone is inspired by and to do different things.

Here's Katie's inspired story:

"Every morning, I'll write one page in my journal," Katie shares. "I keep it to one page, but I don't have any goal for it or structure to it other than to just journal what I feel like journaling that day... it tends to be a frustration or a problem on my mind, usually business-oriented, but it allows me to work through it, and not leave it in my head... I do always end the page with something I am grateful for and appreciate that day."

Every morning, without fail, Katie makes sure not to check her phone until she journals. "This is HUGE," she says. "Doing this keeps my mind in the right place... one email can completely change the trajectory of your thoughts, and I want to hold on to that place I want to."

yay!
you made it,
you've made space for yourself,
you've made time for yourself,
you've made a life of
light-filled mornings,
step by step,
& i'm so proud of you

PART IV
living
light-filled
mornings

Light-filled Mornings are wondrous, because we make them so. Or rather, we've made the space, time, and opportunity to see them as such. It's incredible what can be transformed with the intention to live life to the fullest, starting with each morning we wake up.

The Beginning of Light-filled Mornings

One of the first questions I'm asked when I tell them about light-filled mornings is: How did you think of that?

What's really great is I didn't. It found me, through the process.

As I alluded to in the introduction, I was working through a lot of personal fears that had transformed into health issues several years ago.

I had a host of hormonal issues and was told I had polycystic ovarian syndrome and prescribed hormonal birth control to take care of it—but it didn't take care of it. Instead, my body raged against them, and I felt like I was losing my mind.

Suicidal thoughts that would never have occurred to what I deemed myself to be— a "positive, upbeat" person—were suddenly with me all the time and everything seemed heightened and awful.

I think I gave it 10 days of "trying out" the prescription before I said it had to stop. And I told myself that there had to be another way; and I was so, so very tired of trying to muscle my way through it and figure it out.

I surrendered and hoped.

Books I didn't know I needed started appearing before me—following me in online ads, popping off shelves in bookstores.

Conversations around transforming fears and cultivating faith and taking it one day at a time and opening yourself up to possibility were suddenly all around me.

I had my answer. I also had two small children and a lot of work to do; so I started waking up at 5:30 each morning, because that's what I told myself was necessary to have the time I needed to "save myself." I can laugh about it now, because I see how very well I was at the time. I didn't need saving; I needed to realize that I was already safe.

Years went by, and my life had transformed more than I'd realized it could in my extremely fearful days—it felt transformed, from the inside, regardless of outside circumstances (which had certainly shifted as well).

All the while, I was learning and happy to be learning.

In March of 2018, I was standing in my kitchen nook, my favorite place in my home, and I'd just poured a fresh cup of coffee and could see the steam rising, visibly. I was smiling just because. I was taking deep breaths and appreciating the moment I was in. And I heard it. A nearly-audible voice from the back of my head, swiftly into my right ear: *Light-filled Mornings*.

I felt like the moment stood still. Here was the answer I'd been seeking! It tied it all together. Everything I loved and that mattered to me and that had cultivated a life I'd once dreamed of was because of this feeling, this moment, all of these light-filled mornings strung together. This book has come from it and a host of other adventures; I can't wait to see where Light-filled Mornings leads us next.

Living Light-filled Mornings

Over the past 30 days, you've experienced it yourself:
Being quiet and still and cozy opens you up to a flurry of movement—within and without—which then inspires you to do and be as the one you came into this world to be.

That's where the real magic happens.

It can be as simple as spending that extra time with your morning coffee.

We, as humans, like to make things complicated—but it needn't be so.

To fully live in the magic the morning holds, we just need to let ourselves:
1. See it
2. Breathe it in
3. Be it—because it's really who we are, anyway

I love to serve as a guide, but I really want you to define these for yourself—because we learn so much more through experience than we do with words.

I invite you to have a conversation with your higher self, your intuition, your soul, with God, with a trusted guide of a higher order.

I invite you to ask: ***"How do I live light-filled mornings?"***
And see what flows.
You'll know to trust what comes when it's non-judgmental; feels like a breath of fresh air; and feels true for you, even if your mind wants to question the actual words.

It's also a question that you can ask, any day you feel it needs asking. Your life, your mornings, are living, breathing things that change and evolve, just like you.

Whenever you feel like it's a good time to revisit, remember you can ask again.

For instance, I asked just this morning, while writing this page:
How do I live light-filled mornings?

This is what came to me:
You get out of your own way—by your own, we mean the egoic you, the one that would like to control things, however silly that may be. Because you don't want her in control—you want the one that knows the way in control. The real you.

To get out of your own way, you must first acknowledge the mystery of life—in every morning sunrise, in every drop of rain, in every encounter. And then you must acknowledge that you understand this mystery from a deeper perspective. Indeed, you are part of it. How could you not be?

Living light-filled mornings will mean doing what your heart calls you to, even when it's not convenient. But it is convenient, truly; because it's all that ever is convenient.

Delight in your joy. This is true. This is where the truth lies. In your joy. In doing what lights your way. Like a map with pins in place, the guide is lit for you, the path is lit for you, all you have to do is keep following that next star on the map. Your joy will show you the way. And so, living light-filled mornings becomes a game—a fun game of joy and truth and little winks of surprise.

These are your mornings. Not another task to get done, but a way to live with intention and joy. I am so excited for you, dear friend, to allow this life to thrill you.

Pour yourself another cup of coffee and enjoy.

Mantras to Take With You as You Live Light-filled Mornings

1. I can allow things to be simple.
2. I deserve to live my life joyfully.
3. I can open up and let things flow.
4. When I see things that light me up, I can follow them.
5. The more appreciative I am of my morning, the more there is to appreciate.

Made in the USA
Columbia, SC
28 February 2020